REFLECTIONS

Guide Posts and Images for the Journey

Marvel Elizabeth Harrison, Ph.D.
Terry Kellogg, CCDP

with artwork by

Gregory Michaels

Profits from *REFLECTIONS* are shared with
The Bird's Of Prey Foundation in Coaldale, Alberta, Canada.
In respect for our planet *REFLECTIONS* is printed on recycled paper.

BRAT Publishing, 369 Montezuma, Suite 203, Santa Fe, NM 87501

Copyright ©1994 Marvel E. Harrison
Harrison, Marvel • Kellogg, Terry • Michaels, Greg

ISBN 1-880257-06-8

REFLECTIONS IS DEDICATED TO

THE ARTISTS WHO PORTRAY &
THE ADVENTURERS WHO RELISH &
ALL WHO PROTECT NATURE'S OFFERINGS

Especially our friends

The Artists, **Cary Ennis, Jim Meger, Catharine Stewart-Roache, Elizabeth Berry & Geoff Stalker**

The Adventurers, **Dennis Brandt, Betsy Barnett, Jon Cross, Ron Harrison, Dan Kellogg, Will Steger, Ross Taylor & Merlin Wheeler**

The Protectors, **Robert and Lorene Harrison who are dedicated to the *Bird's Of Prey Center* in Coaldale, Alberta, Canada**

We would also like to acknowledge the support and creative energy of our friends Cary, Dennis & Karen and the flexibility and dedication of Linda.

All of creation is a journey. The life contained within the envelope of earth's atmosphere is also on a journey, the journey of seasonal cycles, of reproducing, the journey from seed to soil.

This journey is enjoyed when we accept the processes of living-our developmental stages of childhood through adulthood, grieving our losses as a process of hurting to healing and embracing the new, the forgiveness process, aging and wisdom, conversion to life and the inspiration of spirituality.

The journey is easier when we discover guideposts that help us with direction and distance so we may pace ourselves without becoming lost. When the guidepost reflects our spirit and strength we are more likely to remain on the path of self becoming. *We wish you a sense of wonder, wisdom and welcome on your journey.*

Wonder is the child like noticing of the miracles of creation we are constantly surrounded by. It is also the ability to wonder about things, the questioning enhances the quest.

Wisdom is the integration of awareness and resources, inward and outward. Our wisdom listens to the voices of past path makers and helps us forge a trail based on other's directions and our own unique adventures.

Welcome is the sense of acceptance, the knowing we are where we belong and we belong where we are going. To be welcome allows us to be us.

As we journey with our companions of wisdom, wonder and welcome we become able to witness for the travels of others, becoming the guide by the example of our journey.

Life is a journey without a destination.
The journey itself is the destination.

The future of the world does not lie in the hands of children,
it lies in the hands that hold the hands of children.
We cannot hold the hands of children until we
hold the hand and
heal the heart of our own childness.

Rituals, though much like elaborate child play,
are the channel to universal meaning.

A moment of touching another's spirit
leaves an eternal imprint on their soul.

Vulnerability is the gift we give to those we trust.

This offering is called love.

The earth is as dependent on us as we are on it.
Our dominion over earth is not
ownership but guardianship.

Our human spark is ignited
when we face the truths of
self with a sense of humor.

Each day the waves wash the beaches
clean of all previous markings in
preparation for our footsteps.

The sounds of wind rustled leaves and
waves somersaulting on beaches are
the applause for our presence.

Intimacy is the sacred relationship
found in a simple act of two
persons accepting it is theirs.

Step out on faith. Growth comes through risk.

When we believe in magic
we can recognize it when it happens.

Anticipation can heighten the moment
while expectations can dampen it.

Visions are blossoms of the mind.
Dreams are wishes from the heart.
Meaning is the music of our soul.
Hope is the seed for tomorrow.

Wisdom is listening to past path makers
who found their way and
left directions for us to follow in
story, legend, myth and song.

Miracles are extraordinary but not out of the ordinary.

Our bodies and feelings hold the forgotten past.

Gratitude nourishes joy.

Boundaries are a construct of identity.

We can't set our limits until we know our limits.
We can't know our limits until we know ourselves.
Once we know ourselves we have our limits.

Our difficulties with ourselves
befall those closest to us.

Without the valleys there would be no peaks.

Without sorrow there would be little joy.

Time heals best when it is shared.

The inward journey allows
outward adventures.

Our loneliness teaches us to
reach toward others.

Our aloneness offers us self friendship.

We are not free to say yes until we can say no.

We are not free to stay until we are free to leave.

The gentle cherishing of all forms of life
comes with accepting life as a single
community sharing the same home and hearth.

An inexhaustible fuel for conflict is embedded fear.

Recreation is the
re-creation of our
mind, body, spirit connection.

Growing up is a child who has gained adulthood,
not an adult who has lost childhood.

The extremes guide us to the middle.
Knowing the middle helps us explore the edges.

Intimacy is the result of a
sharing, caring connection over time.
Friendship, not love or romance maintains intimacy.

Beauty knows no physical bounds.
It radiates from all shapes and sizes.

Noticing beauty is the finest prayer.

Acceptance and serenity is not the
absence of sadness or anger.

Everyday be physically active in a gentle way.

We can't out run or hide from our past.
It is our constant traveling companion.
The journey is smoother when we befriend it.

Life's responsibilities include
noticing, exploration and guardianship.

Tread softly across the vastness of the planet.

Self honesty is the radiant force of our spirit.
Dishonesty is a measure of brokeness.
Honesty comes from facing the truth of self.

R.G. MICHAELS   '92

We can
touch with a word,
caress with a glance and
hold in our hearts.

Happiness comes more from having our
dreams than achieving them.

Play is not about what we do,
        it's our attitude towards what we do.
                Take play seriously and serious playfully.

Values give us value.

The true measure of values is how we
spend our time, energy and creativity.

Anxiety and worry are
windows to the frightened child.

Depression and sadness are
windows to the hurting child.

Impatience and apathy are
windows to the angry child.

Intimacy with others
flows from
intimacy with self.
Identity is self intimacy.

Our darkest times and
deepest losses offer growth and
expansion - the process of soul awakening.

It's not a gray area
between the extremes of
black and white but an
array of all possible colors.

Curiosity and imagination are
deeper sources of learning
than education and teaching.

G.M.

Imagination
is the vehicle for
going beyond possibilities.

What we fantasize, we realize - imagine well!

Life is a mystery
to be embraced
rather than a problem
to be solved.

The most difficult questions
sometimes have the simplest answers.

Simplicity is the path to serenity.
Seek what is genuine, spirited and simple.

Body acceptance has nothing to do with body shape or size.

I don't have a body, I am a body.
When I listen to my body, I listen to myself.
I can celebrate my body.

If we don't have our feelings, our feelings will have us.

There is no healing without the feeling,
no leaving without the grieving.
Grieving fuels the forward movement of our lives.

Our relationships reflect our
connection to creation.

It takes courage to travel alone and
even more to share the journey.

Affirmations are simple noticings reflecting spirit and vitality. Affirm what you cannot photograph.

A sense of humor is not the ability to tell jokes or be funny but rather the ability to laugh at jokes and notice what is humorous.

We are owned by what we own.
Learn loanership rather than ownership.

Friends, families, ideas, property and
experiences are simply on loan to us to
cherish and protect while the
journey is shared.

From our trials we discover our trails.

From our pathos we find our paths.

God deserves a standing ovation.

Applaud God!

Creating our own reality
may not be worth the loneliness.
Sharing reality offers belonging.

Seek guides rather than gurus,
mentors rather than managers,
confidants rather than confessors ,
friends rather than foes.

What we search for we cannot find.
We only find what we embrace.

Creating meaning from experiences gives us purpose and direction.

The meaning of our hurts lies in a deeper ability to witness for others.

RGT. HEINPERS 1992

Laughter is the cement for friendship.
Laugh lines are life lines.
Humor is the soaring spirit of humanity.

The road is smoother when we don't
take ourselves too seriously.

Passion for life enhances all pleasures.
Compassion is living with passion.
Choose compassion as a life force.
Embody compassion.

Our children are not our children,
they are a miracle of the gift of life itself.

We can't embrace the miracle of our children
until we embrace the miracle of ourselves.

Destructive behaviors and relationships are often reactions to or reenactments of unresolved past hurts and losses.

Critical thinking is the balance
between naiveté and criticism.

The ability to question is part of the quest.
Exploring the questions brings more
wisdom than having the answers.

Reduce - Reuse - Recycle

Recycling is not a substitute for consuming less.

Accepting my reality
frees me to change my reality.

Our substance carries us through the
places that shatter appearances.

Life is a flowing river of process and change.

Enjoy the process and accept the change
rather than planning the event and seeking the goal.

Clutter can be physical or mental.
An over structured life has a fragile foundation
when the base is built between appointments.

Truth can be used to embrace or deflate those around us.

Rigid honesty can break a heart.
Rigorous honesty can heal the soul.

The righteous path is seldom the right path.

Needing to be right often results in being left.

Silence allows the hearing of the inner
whispers and beckonings of our true path.

Kindness to strangers creates a benevolent world.
Be especially considerate of those less fortunate.

Life is a freefall.

Some of us are falling through space and time
screaming in terror, filled with anxiety about the landing.

Some of us are falling through space and time
screaming in glee, filled with joy about the journey.

Some of us believe the landing will be a safe
one in the arms of a life source.

Whatever you believe about that
Enjoy the ride!

Marvel Harrison, a native of Canada, is a wilderness enthusiast and an avid runner, skier and canoeist who likes to play. She has a Ph.D. in Counseling Psychology, and is an author, therapist and lecturer specializing in a gentle approach to self acceptance. Marvel's spirit and zest for life are easily felt by audiences everywhere. She makes her home on a canyon in the mountains of northern New Mexico.

Terry Kellogg is a parent, athlete, counselor and teacher. For over twenty years he has been helping families with compulsive and addictive behaviors. Besides writing poetry and playing rugby, he is an insightful therapist and an advocate for vulnerable groups and our planet. Terry is an entertaining, challenging, inspiring, and much sought after speaker. Terry feels most at home in the Boundary Waters of Minnesota or on the pink sand beaches of Harbour Island, Bahamas.

Marvel and Terry, as program consultants to ANACAPA By The Sea in Port Hueneme, California, design and facilitate intensive workshops. They are also directors of the *LifeWorks* and *Life Balance* ™ programs at The Mulberry Center in Evansville, Indiana.

Gregory Michaels is a full time dad and a free lance illustrator. His clever wit and sensitivity to children of all ages are apparent in his work and he has a terrific sense of humor to boot! Greg's work can be enjoyed in numerous children's magazines, the best selling book, *Butterfly Kisses* and is featured in the Prehistoric Journey at the Denver Museum of Natural History. Greg and his family live in Denver, Colorado.

For information about workshops, other books, tapes, greeting cards or art by Marvel, Terry, or Greg, please call or write:

1 800 359-2728
BRAT Publishing, 369 Montezuma, Suite 203, Santa Fe, NM 87501